Square by Square
Granny Afghans

When Carol Holding is the designer, you know your Granny Squares will be something special!

Carol's fresh collection of 12 afghans and one pillow ranges from sophisticated textures to wild romps in color. In these pages, you'll find plenty of warm and decorative lap throws and a selection of cuddly baby blankets. And since these designs are made one square at a time, you can take them along wherever you go. They're the perfect projects for today's busy crocheter!

About the Designer

Ask Carol Holding how she feels about crochet, and she says, "I'm obsessed! While I'm making one project, I'm thinking, 'Well, what if I did it this way, instead?' The ideas never stop coming. I taught myself to crochet, starting when I was about eighteen, and I haven't stopped. I also like to paint landscapes. Being creative is natural for me, and that includes home improvement."

Carol and her twin sister currently share a house in South Carolina. Carol says, "I have the bottom floor, and my sister has the top floor. We've worked to get our living spaces the way we want them, but we've recently decided we would rather live farther out in the country. So now we're remodeling a home out in the woods. It's a lot of work, and I really love it, even though I plan on it being the last house I do. But I'll never stop crocheting. I crochet every day, and I'm always thinking of the next design."

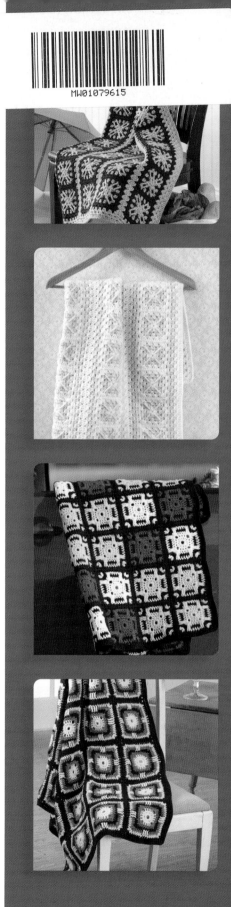

Contents

LEISURE ARTS, INC.
Little Rock, Arkansas

LEISURE ARTS®
the art of everyday living
www.leisurearts.com

MW01079615

Bright Idea

Finished Size: 43" w x 51" l (109 x 129.5) cm

MATERIALS

Medium Weight Yarn **MEDIUM 4**
[7 ounces, 364 yards
    (198 grams, 333 meters) per skein]:
    Hot Pink - 5 skeins
    White - 2 skeins
Crochet hook, size F (3.75 mm) **or** size needed
    for gauge
Tapestry needle

GAUGE: Each Motif = 2$\frac{1}{4}$" (5.75 cm)
            Square = 8" (20.5 cm)

STITCH GUIDE

FRONT POST DOUBLE TREBLE CROCHET
    (abbreviated FPdtr)
YO 3 times, insert hook from **front** to **back**
around post of st indicated *(Fig. 1, page 34)*,
YO and pull up a loop (5 loops on hook), (YO
and draw through 2 loops on hook) 4 times.

SQUARE (Make 30)

MOTIF (Make 4)

With Hot Pink, ch 5; join with slip st to form a ring.

Rnd 1 (Right side)**:** Ch 3 **(counts as first dc, now and throughout)**, 3 dc in ring, (ch 3, 4 dc in ring) 3 times, ch 1, hdc in first dc to form last sp: 16 dc and 4 ch-3 sps.

Loop a short piece of yarn around any stitch to mark Rnd 1 as **right** side.

Rnd 2: Ch 3, (3 dc, ch 3, 4 dc) in same sp, ★ ch 1, skip next 4 dc, (4 dc, ch 3, 4 dc) in next ch-3 sp; repeat from ★ 2 times **more**, ch 1; join with slip st to first dc, finish off.

With Hot Pink, whipstitch Motifs together forming 2 vertical strips of 2 Motifs each *(Fig. 3, page 34)*, beginning in center ch of first corner and ending in center ch of next corner; then whipstitch strips together in same manner forming a square.

BORDER

Rnd 1: With **right** side facing, join White with slip st in any corner ch-3 sp; ch 3, 3 dc in same sp, ch 1, skip next 4 dc, 4 dc in next ch-1 sp, ch 1, skip next 4 dc, 2 dc in next ch-sp, skip joining, 2 dc in next ch-sp, ch 1, skip next 4 dc, 4 dc in next ch-1 sp, ★ ch 1, skip next 4 dc, (4 dc, ch 3, 4 dc) in corner ch-3 sp, ch 1, skip next 4 dc, 4 dc in next ch-1 sp, ch 1, skip next 4 dc, 2 dc in next ch-sp, skip joining, 2 dc in next ch-sp, ch 1, skip next 4 dc, 4 dc in next ch-1 sp; repeat from ★ 2 times **more**, ch 1, skip last 4 dc, 4 dc in same sp as first dc, ch 1, hdc in first dc to form last sp.

Rnd 2: Ch 3, 3 dc in same sp, (ch 1, skip next 4 dc, 4 dc in next ch-1 sp) 4 times, ★ ch 1, skip next 4 dc, (4 dc, ch 3, 4 dc) in corner ch-3 sp, (ch 1, skip next 4 dc, 4 dc in next ch-1 sp) 4 times; repeat from ★ 2 times **more**, ch 1, skip last 4 dc, 4 dc in same sp as first dc, ch 3; join with slip st to first dc, finish off.

Rnd 3: With **right** side facing, join Hot Pink with slip st in any corner ch-3 sp; ch 3, 3 dc in same sp, ★ † ch 1, skip next 4 dc, dc in next ch-1 sp, work FPdtr around second dc of 4-dc group **below** same ch-1 sp, work FPdtr around next dc, dc in same ch-1 sp on Rnd 2, (ch 1, skip next 4 dc, 4 dc in next ch-1 sp) 3 times, ch 1, skip next 4 dc, dc in next ch-1 sp, work FPdtr around second dc of 4-dc group **below** same ch-1 sp, work FPdtr around next dc, dc in same ch-1 sp on Rnd 2, ch 1, skip next 4 dc †, (4 dc, ch 3, 4 dc) in corner ch-3 sp; repeat from ★ 2 times **more**, then repeat from † to † once, 4 dc in same sp as first dc, ch 1, hdc in first dc to form last sp.

Rnd 4: Ch 3, 3 dc in same sp, (ch 1, skip next 4 sts, 4 dc in next ch-1 sp) 6 times, ★ ch 1, skip next 4 dc, (4 dc, ch 3, 4 dc) in corner ch-3 sp, (ch 1, skip next 4 sts, 4 dc in next ch-1 sp) 6 times; repeat from ★ 2 times **more**, ch 1, skip last 4 dc, 4 dc in same sp as first dc, ch 3; join with slip st to first dc, finish off.

ASSEMBLY

With Hot Pink, whipstitch Squares together forming 5 vertical strips of 6 Squares each, beginning in center ch of first corner and ending in center ch of next corner; then whipstitch strips together in same manner.

3

Instructions continued on page 9

Little Boy Blue

 **EASY**

Finished Size: 33" w x 37½" l (84 x 95.5) cm

MATERIALS

Medium Weight Yarn **4**
[7 ounces, 364 yards
    (198 grams, 333 meters) per skein].
Lt Blue - 3 skeins
White - 1 skein
Crochet hook, size F (3.75 mm) **or** size needed
    for gauge
Tapestry needle

GAUGE: Each Square = 4½" (11.5 cm)

STITCH GUIDE

BEGINNING CLUSTER (uses one sp)
Ch 2, YO, insert hook in sp indicated, YO and
pull up a loop, YO and draw through 2 loops
on hook, YO, insert hook in **same** sp, YO and
pull up a loop, YO and draw through 2 loops on
hook, YO and draw through all 3 loops on hook.

CLUSTER (uses one sp)
YO, insert hook in sp indicated, YO and pull
up a loop, YO and draw through 2 loops on
hook, ★ YO, insert hook in **same** sp, YO and
pull up a loop, YO and draw through 2 loops on
hook; repeat from ★ once **more**, YO and draw
through all 4 loops on hook.

FRONT POST DOUBLE TREBLE CROCHET
  (abbreviated FPdtr)

YO 3 times, insert hook from **front** to **back**
around post of st indicated **(Fig. 1, page 34)**,
YO and pull up a loop (5 loops on hook), (YO
and draw through 2 loops on hook) 4 times.
Skip st behind FPdtr.

SQUARE (Make 56)

With Lt Blue, ch 6; join with slip st to form a ring.

Rnd 1 (Right side)**:** Work (Beginning Cluster,
ch 2, Cluster) in ring, ★ ch 4, work (Cluster, ch 2,
Cluster) in ring; repeat from ★ 2 times **more**, ch 2,
hdc in top of Beginning Cluster to form last sp:
8 Clusters, 4 ch-4 sps, and 4 ch-2 sps.

Loop a short piece of yarn around any stitch to
mark Rnd 1 as **right** side.

Rnd 2: Work Beginning Cluster in same sp, ch 2,
3 dc in next ch-2 sp, ★ ch 2, work (Cluster, ch 2,
Cluster) in next ch-4 sp, ch 2, 3 dc in next ch-2 sp;
repeat from ★ 2 times **more**, ch 2, work Cluster
in same sp as first st, ch 2; join with slip st to
Beginning Cluster, finish off.

Rnd 3: With **right** side facing, join White with
slip st in any corner ch-2 sp (between Clusters);
ch 3 **(counts as first dc, now and throughout)**,
(2 dc, ch 2, 3 dc) in same sp, 2 dc in next ch-2 sp,
dc in next 3 dc, 2 dc in next ch-2 sp, ★ (3 dc, ch 2,
3 dc) in next ch-2 sp, 2 dc in next ch-2 sp, dc in
next 3 dc, 2 dc in next ch-2 sp; repeat from ★
2 times **more**; join with slip st to first dc, finish off.

Rnd 4: With **right** side facing, join Lt Blue with
slip st in any corner ch-2 sp; ch 3, (2 dc, ch 2,
3 dc) in same sp, skip next dc, dc in next 3 dc,
work FPdtr around first dc of 3-dc group on Rnd 2,
(dc in next dc, work FPdtr around next dc of
3-dc group on Rnd 2) twice, dc in next 3 dc,
★ skip next dc, (3 dc, ch 2, 3 dc) in next ch-2 sp,
skip next dc, dc in next 3 dc, work FPdtr around
first dc of 3-dc group on Rnd 2, (dc in next dc,
work FPdtr around next dc of 3-dc group on
Rnd 2) twice, dc in next 3 dc; repeat from ★
2 times **more**, skip last dc; join with slip st to first
dc, finish off.

 Instructions continued on page 9

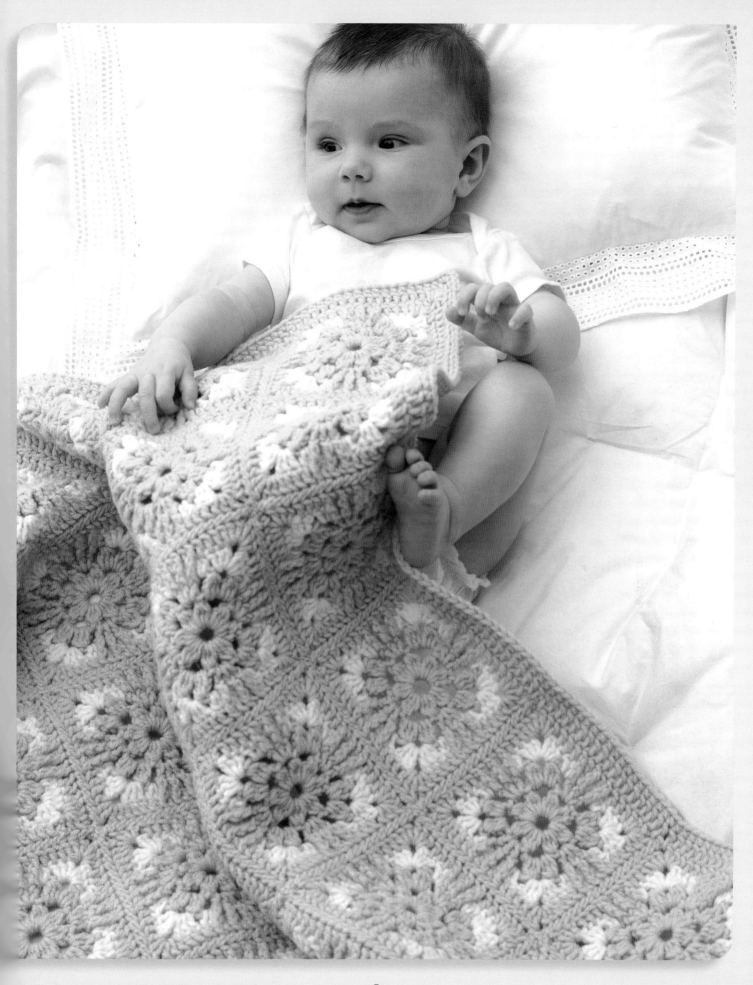

Sea Breeze Set

Finished Size:
Afghan: 39" w x 53$\frac{1}{4}$" l (99 x 135) cm
Pillow: 15" (38 cm) square

MATERIALS

Medium Weight Yarn **(4)** MEDIUM
[7 ounces, 364 yards
    (198 grams, 333 meters) per skein]:
    Turquoise - 3 skeins
    Variegated - 2 skeins
    White - 2 skeins
[5 ounces, 232 yards (141 grams, 212 meters)
    per skein]:
    Lime - 3 skeins
Crochet hook, size F (3.75 mm) **or** size needed
    for gauge
15" (38 cm) Pillow form
Tapestry needle

GAUGE: Each Square = 4$\frac{3}{4}$" (12 cm)

AFGHAN
SQUARE (Make 88)

With Variegated, ch 5; join with slip st to form
a ring.

Rnd 1 (Right side)**:** Ch 3 **(counts as first dc, now
and throughout)**, 3 dc in ring, (ch 3, 4 dc in ring)
3 times, ch 3; join with slip st to first dc, finish off:
16 dc and 4 ch-3 sps.

Loop a short piece of yarn around any stitch to
mark Rnd 1 as **right** side.

Rnd 2: With **right** side facing, join White with
slip st in any corner ch-3 sp, ch 3, (3 dc, ch 3,
4 dc) in same sp, ★ ch 1, (4 dc, ch 3, 4 dc) in next
ch-3 sp; repeat from ★ 2 times **more**, ch 1; join
with slip st to first dc, finish off.

Rnd 3: With **right** side facing, join Lime with
slip st in any corner ch-3 sp, ch 3, (3 dc, ch 3,
4 dc) in same sp, ch 1, 4 dc in next ch-1 sp,
★ ch 1, (4 dc, ch 3, 4 dc) in next ch-3 sp, ch 1,
4 dc in next ch-1 sp; repeat from ★ 2 times **more**,
ch 1; join with slip st to first dc, finish off.

Rnd 4: With **right** side facing, join Turquoise with
slip st in any corner ch-3 sp; ch 3, (3 dc, ch 3,
4 dc) in same sp, (ch 1, 4 dc in next ch-1 sp) twice,
★ ch 1, (4 dc, ch 3, 4 dc) in corner ch-3 sp, (ch 1,
4 dc in next ch-1 sp) twice; repeat from ★ 2 times
more, ch 1; join with slip st to first dc, finish off.

ASSEMBLY

With Turquoise, whipstitch Squares together
forming 8 vertical strips of 11 Squares each
(Fig. 3, page 34), beginning in center ch of first
corner and ending in center ch of next corner;
then whipstitch strips together in same manner.

BORDER

Rnd 1: With **right** side facing, join Turquoise with slip st in any corner ch-3 sp; ch 3, (3 dc, ch 3, 4 dc) in same sp, (ch 1, 4 dc in next ch-1 sp) 3 times, ch 1, † 4 dc in joining, (ch 1, 4 dc in next ch-1 sp) 3 times, ch 1 †, repeat from † to † across to next corner ch-3 sp, ★ (4 dc, ch 3, 4 dc) in corner ch-3 sp, (ch 1, 4 dc in next ch-1 sp) 3 times, ch 1, repeat from † to † across to next corner ch-3 sp; repeat from ★ 2 times **more**; join with slip st to first dc.

Rnd 2: Ch 1, sc in same st and in next 3 dc, 3 sc in corner ch-3 sp, ★ sc in each dc and in each ch-1 sp across to next corner ch-3 sp, 3 sc in corner ch-3 sp; repeat from ★ 2 times **more**, sc in each dc and in each ch-1 sp across; join with slip st to first sc, finish off.

PILLOW
FRONT
SQUARE (Make 4)

Work same as Afghan Square.

ASSEMBLY

With Turquoise, whipstitch Squares together forming 2 vertical strips of 2 Squares each **(Fig. 3, page 34)**, beginning in center ch of first corner and ending in center ch of next corner; then whipstitch strips together in same manner forming a Square.

Instructions continued on page 8

BORDER

Rnd 1: With **right** side facing, join Turquoise with slip st in any corner ch-3 sp; ch 3, (3 dc, ch 3, 4 dc) in same sp, (ch 1, 4 dc in next ch-1 sp) 3 times, ch 1, 2 dc in next ch-sp, skip joining, 2 dc in next ch-sp, (ch 1, 4 dc in next ch-1 sp) 3 times, ★ ch 1, (4 dc, ch 3, 4 dc) in corner ch-3 sp, (ch 1, 4 dc in next ch-1 sp) 3 times, ch 1, 2 dc in next ch-sp, skip joining, 2 dc in next ch-sp, (ch 1, 4 dc in next ch-1 sp) 3 times; repeat from ★ 2 times **more**, ch 1; join with slip st to first dc, finish off.

Rnd 2: With **right** side facing, join White with slip st in any corner ch-3 sp; ch 3, (3 dc, ch 3, 4 dc) in same sp, (ch 1, 4 dc in next ch-1 sp) 8 times, ★ ch 1, (4 dc, ch 3, 4 dc) in corner ch-3 sp, (ch 1, 4 dc in next ch-1 sp) 8 times; repeat from ★ 2 times **more**, ch 1; join with slip st to first dc, finish off.

Rnd 3: With **right** side facing, join Lime with slip st in any corner ch-3 sp; ch 3, (3 dc, ch 3, 4 dc) in same sp, (ch 1, 4 dc in next ch-1 sp) 9 times, ★ ch 1, (4 dc, ch 3, 4 dc) in corner ch-3 sp, (ch 1, 4 dc in next ch-1 sp) 9 times; repeat from ★ 2 times **more**, ch 1; join with slip st to first dc, finish off.

Rnd 4: With **right** side facing, join Turquoise with slip st in any corner ch-3 sp; ch 3, 3 dc in same sp, (ch 1, 4 dc in next ch-1 sp) 10 times, ★ ch 1, (4 dc, ch 3, 4 dc) in corner ch-3 sp, (ch 1, 4 dc in next ch-1 sp) 10 times; repeat from ★ 2 times **more**, ch 1, 4 dc in same sp as first st, ch 1, hdc in first dc to form last sp.

Rnd 5: Ch 3, 3 dc in same sp, (ch 1, 4 dc in next ch-1 sp) 11 times, ★ ch 1, (4 dc, ch 3, 4 dc) in corner ch-3 sp, (ch 1, 4 dc in next ch-1 sp) 11 times; repeat from ★ 2 times **more**, ch 1, 4 dc in same sp as first st, ch 3; join with slip st to first dc.

Rnd 6: Ch 1, sc in same st, ★ sc in each dc and in each ch-1 sp across to corner ch-3 sp, 5 sc in corner ch-3 sp; repeat from ★ 3 times **more**; join with slip st to first sc, finish off.

BACK

With Variegated, ch 5; join with slip st to form a ring.

Rnd 1 (Right side): Ch 3, 3 dc in ring, (ch 3, 4 dc in ring) 3 times, ch 1, hdc in first dc to form last sp: 16 dc and 4 ch-3 sps.

Mark Rnd 1 as **right** side.

Rnd 2: Ch 3, 3 dc in same sp, ★ ch 1, (4 dc, ch 3, 4 dc) in next ch-3 sp; repeat from ★ 2 times **more**, ch 1, 4 dc in same sp as first st, ch 1, hdc in first dc to form last sp: 32 dc, 4 ch-3 sps, and 4 ch-1 sps.

Rnd 3: Ch 3, 3 dc in same sp, ch 1, 4 dc in next ch-1 sp, ★ ch 1, (4 dc, ch 3, 4 dc) in corner ch-3 sp, ch 1, 4 dc in next ch-1 sp; repeat from ★ 2 times **more**, ch 1, 4 dc in same sp as first st, ch 1, hdc in first dc to form last sp: 48 dc, 4 ch-3 sps, and 8 ch-1 sps.

Rnd 4: Ch 3, 3 dc in same sp, (ch 1, 4 dc in next ch-1 sp) twice, ★ ch 1, (4 dc, ch 3, 4 dc) in corner ch-3 sp, (ch 1, 4 dc in next ch-1 sp) twice; repeat from ★ 2 times **more**, ch 1, 4 dc in same sp as first st, ch 1, hdc in first dc to form last sp: 64 dc, 4 ch-3 sps, and 12 ch-1 sps.

Rnds 5-12: Ch 3, 3 dc in same sp, (ch 1, 4 dc in next ch-1 sp) across to next corner ch-3 sp, ★ ch 1, (4 dc, ch 3, 4 dc) in corner ch-3 sp, (ch 1, 4 dc in next ch-1 sp) across to next corner ch-3 sp; repeat from ★ 2 times **more**, ch 1, 4 dc in same sp as first st, ch 1, hdc in first dc to form last sp.

Rnd 13: Ch 3, 3 dc in same sp, (ch 1, 4 dc in next ch-1 sp) across to next corner ch-3 sp, ★ ch 1, (4 dc, ch 3, 4 dc) in corner ch-3 sp, (ch 1, 4 dc in next ch-1 sp) across to next corner ch-3 sp; repeat from ★ 2 times **more**, ch 1, 4 dc in same sp as first st, ch 3; join with slip st to first dc.

Rnd 14: Ch 1, sc in same st, ★ sc in each dc and in each ch-1 sp across to corner ch-3 sp, 5 sc in corner ch-3 sp; repeat from ★ 3 times **more**; join with slip st to first sc, finish off.

FINISHING

With Turquoise and matching stitches, whipstitch Front to Back, inserting Pillow form before closing.

Bright Idea

Instructions continued from page 3

OUTER BORDER

Rnd 1: With **right** side facing, join Hot Pink with slip st in any corner ch-3 sp; ch 3, (3 dc, ch 3, 4 dc) in same sp, ★ (ch 1, skip next 4 dc, 4 dc in next ch-1 sp) 7 times, † ch 1, skip next 4 dc, 2 dc in next ch-sp, skip joining, 2 dc in next ch-sp, (ch 1, skip next 4 dc, 4 dc in next ch-1 sp) 7 times ch 1 †, repeat from † to † across to next corner ch-3 sp, (4 dc, ch 3, 4 dc) in next corner ch-3 sp; repeat from ★ 2 times **more**, (ch 1, skip next 4 dc, 4 dc in next ch-1 sp) 7 times, repeat from † to † across, skip last 4 dc; join with slip st to first dc.

Rnd 2: Ch 1, sc in same st and in next 3 dc, 3 sc in corner ch-3 sp, ★ sc in each dc and in each ch-1 sp across to next corner ch-3 sp, 3 sc in corner ch-3 sp; repeat from ★ 2 times **more**, sc in each dc and in each ch-1 sp across; join with slip st to first sc, finish off.

Little Boy Blue

Instructions continued from page 4

ASSEMBLY

With Lt Blue, whipstitch Squares together, forming 7 vertical strips of 8 Squares each *(Fig. 3, page 34)*, beginning in second ch of first corner and ending in first ch of next corner; then whipstitch strips together in same manner.

BORDER

Rnd 1: With **right** side facing, join Lt Blue with slip st in any corner ch-2 sp; ch 3, (2 dc, ch 2, 3 dc) in same sp, ★ † skip next dc, (dc in each st across to next ch-sp, dc in ch-sp, skip joining, dc in ch-sp on next Square) across to last Square before corner, dc in each st across to within one dc of corner ch-2 sp, skip next dc †, (3 dc, ch 2, 3 dc) in corner ch-2 sp; repeat from ★ 2 times **more**, then repeat from † to † once; join with slip st to first dc.

Rnd 2: Ch 1, sc in same st and in next 2 dc, 3 sc in corner ch-2 sp, ★ sc in each dc across to next corner ch-2 sp, 3 sc in corner ch-2 sp; repeat from ★ 2 times **more**, sc in each dc across; join with slip st to first sc, finish off.

Red Delicious

Finished Size: 39" w x 50" l (99 x 127) cm

MATERIALS

Medium Weight Yarn
[7 ounces, 364 yards
   (198 grams, 333 meters) per skein]:
   Red - 5 skeins
   Tan - 3 skeins
Crochet hook, size F (3.75 mm) **or** size needed
   for gauge
Tapestry needle

GAUGE: Each Square = 3³/₄" (9.5 cm)

STITCH GUIDE

BEGINNING CLUSTER (uses one sp)
Ch 2, YO, insert hook in sp indicated, YO and
pull up a loop, YO and draw through 2 loops on
hook, YO, insert hook in **same** sp, YO and pull
up a loop, YO and draw through 2 loops on
hook, YO and draw through all 3 loops on
hook.

CLUSTER (uses one sp)
YO, insert hook in sp indicated, YO and pull up
a loop, YO and draw through 2 loops on hook,
★ YO, insert hook in **same** sp, YO and pull up
a loop, YO and draw through 2 loops on hook;
repeat from ★ once **more**, YO and draw
through all 4 loops on hook.

SQUARE (Make 130)

With Tan, ch 6; join with slip st to form a ring.

Rnd 1 (Right side)**:** Work (Beginning Cluster, ch 2,
Cluster) in ring, ★ ch 4, work (Cluster, ch 2,
Cluster) in ring; repeat from ★ 2 times **more**, ch 2,
hdc in top of Beginning Cluster to form last sp:
8 Clusters, 4 ch-4 sps, and 4 ch-2 sps.

Loop a short piece of yarn around any stitch to
mark Rnd 1 as **right** side.

Rnd 2: Work Beginning Cluster in same sp, ch 2,
3 dc in next ch-2 sp, ★ ch 2, work (Cluster, ch 2,
Cluster) in next ch-4 sp, ch 2, 3 dc in next ch-2 sp;
repeat from ★ 2 times **more**, ch 2, work Cluster in
same sp as first st, ch 2; join with slip st to
Beginning Cluster, finish off.

Rnd 3: With **right** side facing, join Red with slip st
in any corner ch-2 sp (between Clusters); work
(Beginning Cluster, ch 2, Cluster) in same sp, ch 2,
2 dc in next ch-2 sp, dc in next 3 dc, 2 dc in next
ch-2 sp, ★ ch 2, work (Cluster, ch 2, Cluster) in
next ch-2 sp, ch 2, 2 dc in next ch-2 sp, dc in next
3 dc, 2 dc in next ch-2 sp; repeat from ★ 2 times
more, ch 2; join with slip st to Beginning Cluster.

Rnd 4: Ch 1, sc in same st, (2 sc, ch 1, 2 sc) in
corner ch-2 sp, sc in next st, 2 sc in next ch-2 sp,
sc in next 7 dc, 2 sc in next ch-2 sp, ★ sc in next
st, (2 sc, ch 1, 2 sc) in corner ch-2 sp, sc in next st,
2 sc in next ch-2 sp, sc in next 7 dc, 2 sc in next
ch-2 sp; repeat from ★ 2 times **more**; join with
slip st to first sc, finish off.

ASSEMBLY

With Red, whipstitch Squares together, forming 10 vertical strips of 13 Squares each *(Fig. 3, page 34)*, beginning in ch of first corner and ending in ch of next corner; then whipstitch strips together in same manner.

BORDER

Rnd 1: With **right** side facing, join Red with slip st in second sc to **right** of any corner ch-1 sp; ch 3 **(counts as first dc)**, 2 dc in next sc, ch 1, 2 dc in next sc, ★ dc in next sc and in each st and joining across to within one sc of next corner ch-1 sp, 2 dc in next sc, ch 1, 2 dc in next sc; repeat from ★ 2 times **more**, dc in next sc and in each st and joining across; join with slip st to first dc.

Rnd 2: Ch 1, sc in same st and in next 2 dc, 3 sc in corner ch-1 sp, ★ sc in each dc across to next corner ch-1 sp, 3 sc in corner ch-1 sp; repeat from ★ 2 times **more**, sc in each dc across; join with slip st to first sc, finish off.

City Blocks

■■■□ **INTERMEDIATE**

Finished Size: 41¹/₂" w x 53¹/₂" l (105.5 x 136) cm

MATERIALS

Medium Weight Yarn (4)

[7 ounces, 364 yards
    (198 grams, 333 meters) per skein]:
    Dk Brown - 4 skeins
    Lt Blue - 2 skeins
Crochet hook, size F (3.75 mm) **or** size needed
    for gauge
Tapestry needle

GAUGE: Each Square = 4" (10 cm)

SOLID SQUARE (Make 52)

With Dk Brown, ch 10; join with slip st to form a ring.

Rnd 1 (Right side)**:** Ch 4 **(counts as first dc plus ch 1)**, (dc in ring, ch 1) 15 times; join with slip st to first dc: 16 dc and 16 ch-1 sps.

Loop a short piece of yarn around any stitch to mark Rnd 1 as **right** side.

Rnd 2: Slip st in first ch-1 sp, ch 6 **(counts as first dc plus ch 3)**, ★ dc in next ch-1 sp, (ch 1, dc in next ch-1 sp) 3 times, ch 3; repeat from ★ 2 times **more**, (dc in next ch-1 sp, ch 1) 3 times; join with slip st to first dc.

Rnd 3: Slip st in first ch-3 sp, ch 3 **(counts as first dc, now and throughout)**, (3 dc, ch 2, 4 dc) in same sp, (ch 1, dc in next ch-1 sp) 3 times, ch 1, ★ (4 dc, ch 2, 4 dc) in next ch-3 sp, (ch 1, dc in next ch-1 sp) 3 times, ch 1; repeat from ★ 2 times **more**; join with slip st to first dc.

Rnd 4: Ch 3, dc in next 2 dc, skip next dc, (2 dc, ch 3, 2 dc) in corner ch-3 sp, skip next dc, dc in next 3 dc, (ch 1, dc in next dc) 3 times, ch 1, ★ dc in next 3 dc, skip next dc, (2 dc, ch 3, 2 dc) in corner ch-3 sp, skip next dc, dc in next 3 dc, (ch 1, dc in next dc) 3 times, ch 1; repeat from ★ 2 times **more**; join with slip st to first dc, finish off.

2-COLOR SQUARE (Make 78)

With Lt Blue, work same as Solid Square through Rnd 3; finish off.

Rnd 4: With **right** side facing, join Dk Brown with slip st in any corner ch-2 sp; ch 3, (dc, ch 3, 2 dc) in same sp, skip next dc, dc in next 3 dc, (ch 1, dc in next dc) 3 times, ch 1, dc in next 3 dc, ★ skip next dc, (2 dc, ch 3, 2 dc) in corner ch-3 sp, skip next dc, dc in next 3 dc, (ch 1, dc in next dc) 3 times, ch 1, dc in next 3 dc; repeat from ★ 2 times **more**, skip last dc; join with slip st to first dc, finish off.

ASSEMBLY

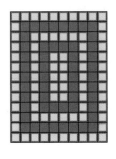

With Dk Brown and using Placement Diagram as a guide (see right), whipstitch Squares together forming 10 vertical strips of 13 Squares each **(Fig. 3, page 34)**, beginning in center ch of first corner and ending in center ch of next corner; then whipstitch strips together in same manner.

Instructions continued on page 19

Star Spangled

Finished Size:
43¹/₂" w x 50¹/₂" l (110.5 x 128.5) cm

MATERIALS

Medium Weight Yarn
[7 ounces, 364 yards
    (198 grams, 333 meters) per skein]:
    Red - 5 skeins
    Blue - 2 skeins
    White - 1 skein
Crochet hook, size F (3.75 mm) **or** size needed
    for gauge
Tapestry needle

GAUGE: Each Square = 5¹/₂" (14 cm)

STITCH GUIDE

BEGINNING CLUSTER (uses one sp)
Ch 2, YO, insert hook in sp indicated, YO and pull up a loop, YO and draw through 2 loops on hook, YO, insert hook in **same** sp, YO and pull up a loop, YO and draw through 2 loops on hook, YO and draw through all 3 loops on hook.

CLUSTER (uses one sp)
YO, insert hook in sp indicated, YO and pull up a loop, YO and draw through 2 loops on hook, ★ YO, insert hook in **same** sp, YO and pull up a loop, YO and draw through 2 loops on hook; repeat from ★ once **more**, YO and draw through all 4 loops on hook.

FRONT POST DOUBLE TREBLE CROCHET
  (abbreviated FPtr)
YO 3 times, insert hook from **front** to **back** around post of st indicated **(Fig. 1, page 34)**, YO and pull up a loop (5 loops on hook), (YO and draw through 2 loops on hook) 4 times. Skip st behind FPdtr.

FRONT POST TREBLE CROCHET
  (abbreviated FPtr)
YO 2 times, insert hook from **front** to **back** around post of st indicated **(Fig. 1, page 34)**, YO and pull up a loop (4 loops on hook), (YO and draw through 2 loops on hook) 3 times. Skip st behind FPdtr.

SQUARE (Make 72)

With Red, ch 6; join with slip st to form a ring.

Rnd 1 (Right side)**:** Work (Beginning Cluster, ch 2, Cluster) in ring, ★ ch 4, work (Cluster, ch 2, Cluster) in ring; repeat from ★ 2 times **more**, ch 4; join with slip to to Beginning Cluster, finish off: 8 Clusters, 4 ch-4 sps, and 4 ch-2 sps.

Loop a short piece of yarn around any stitch to mark Rnd 1 as **right** side.

Rnd 2: With **right** side facing, join White with slip st in any corner ch-4 sp; work (Beginning Cluster, ch 2, Cluster) in same sp, ch 2, 3 dc in next ch-2 sp, ★ ch 2, work (Cluster, ch 2, Cluster) in next ch-4 sp, ch 2, 3 dc in next ch-3 sp; repeat from ★ 2 times **more**, ch 2; join with slip st to Beginning Cluster, finish off.

Rnd 3: With **right** side facing, join Blue with slip st in any corner ch-2 sp (between Clusters); work (Beginning Cluster, ch 2, Cluster) in same sp, ch 2, 2 dc in next ch-2 sp, dc in next 3 dc, 2 dc in next ch-2 sp, ★ ch 2, work (Cluster, ch 2, Cluster) in next ch-2 sp, ch 2, 2 dc in next ch-2 sp, dc in next 3 dc, 2 dc in next ch-2 sp; repeat from ★ 2 times **more**, ch 2; join with slip st to Beginning Cluster, finish off.

Rnd 4: With **right** side facing, join Red with slip st in any corner ch-2 sp; work (Beginning Cluster, ch 2, Cluster) in same sp, ch 1, 2 dc in next ch-2 sp, dc in next 3 dc, work FPdtr around dc **below** next dc, dc in next 3 dc, 2 dc in next ch-2 sp, ★ ch 1, work (Cluster, ch 2, Cluster) in corner ch-2 sp, ch 1, 2 dc in next ch-2 sp, dc in next 3 dc, work FPdtr around dc **below** next dc, dc in next 3 dc, 2 dc in next ch-2 sp; repeat from ★ 2 times **more**, ch 1; join with slip st to Beginning Cluster, finish off.

Instructions continued on page 19

Evergreen

■■■▢▢ **INTERMEDIATE**

Finished Size: 41¹/₂" w x 53¹/₂" l (105.5 x 136) cm

MATERIALS

Medium Weight Yarn
[7 ounces, 364 yards
    (198 grams, 333 meters) per skein**]**·
    Tan - 4 skeins
    Dk Green - 3 skeins
Crochet hook, size F (3.75 mm) **or** size needed
    for gauge
Tapestry needle

GAUGE: Each Square = 4¹/₄" (10.75 cm)

STITCH GUIDE

FRONT POST DOUBLE TREBLE CROCHET
(abbreviated FPdtr)
YO 3 times, insert hook from **front** to **back**
around post of st indicated *(Fig. 1, page 34)*,
YO and pull up a loop (5 loops on hook), (YO
and draw through 2 loops on hook) 4 times.

SQUARE (Make 88)

With Tan, ch 4; join with slip st to form a ring.

Rnd 1 (Right side)**:** Ch 3 **(count as first dc, now
and throughout)**, 2 dc in ring, (ch 1, 3 dc in ring)
3 times, sc in first dc to form last sp.

Loop a short piece of yarn around any stitch to
mark Rnd 1 as **right** side.

Rnd 2: Ch 3, 2 dc in same sp, (3 dc, ch 1, 3 dc) in
each of next 3 ch-1 sps, 3 dc in same sp as first st,
ch 1; join with slip st to first dc, finish off.

Rnd 3: With **right** side facing, join Dk Green with
slip st in any corner ch-1 sp; ch 3, (2 dc, ch 1,
3 dc) in same sp, skip next 3 dc, 3 dc in sp **before**
next dc *(Fig. 2, page 34)*, ★ skip next 3 dc, (3 dc,
ch 1, 3 dc) in next ch-1 sp, skip next 3 dc, 3 dc in
sp **before** next dc; repeat from ★ 2 times **more**,
skip last 3 dc; join with slip st to first dc, finish off.

Rnd 4: With **right** side facing, join Tan with slip st
in any corner ch-1 sp; ch 3, work FPdtr around
second dc to **left** of corner ch-1 sp on Rnd 2, dc in
same sp on Rnd 3, (skip next 3 dc, 3 dc in sp
before next dc) twice, skip next 3 dc, dc in next
corner ch-1 sp, work FPdtr around second dc to
right of corresponding corner ch-1 sp on Rnd 2,
★ (dc, ch 1, dc) in same sp on Rnd 3, work FPdtr
around second dc to **left** of corresponding ch-1 sp
on Rnd 2, dc in same sp on Rnd 3, (skip next 3 dc,
3 dc in sp **before** next dc) twice, skip next 3 dc, dc
in next corner ch-1 sp, work FPdtr around second
dc to **right** of corresponding corner ch-1 sp on
Rnd 2; repeat from ★ 2 times **more**, dc in same sp
on Rnd 3, ch 1; join with slip st to first dc, finish off.

Rnd 5: With **right** side facing, join Dk Green with
slip st in any corner ch-1 sp; ch 3, (2 dc, ch 1,
3 dc) in same sp, (skip next 3 sts, 3 dc in sp
before next dc) 3 times, ★ skip next 3 sts, (3 dc,
ch 1, 3 dc) in next ch-1 sp, (skip next 3 sts, 3 dc in
sp **before** next dc) 3 times; repeat from ★ 2 times
more, skip last 3 dc; join with slip st to first dc,
finish off.

STRIP ASSEMBLY

With Dk Green, whipstitch Squares together, forming 8 vertical strips of 11 Squares each **(Fig. 3, page 34)**, beginning in ch of first corner and ending in ch of next corner.

STRIP BORDER

Rnd 1: With **right** side facing and holding Strip vertically, join Dk Green with slip st in top right corner ch-1 sp; ch 3, (2 dc, ch 1, 3 dc) in same sp, † (skip next 3 dc, 3 dc in sp **before** next dc) 4 times, skip next 3 dc, (3 dc, ch 1, 3 dc) in corner ch-1 sp, (skip next 3 sts, 3 dc in sp **before** next dc) 4 times, ★ skip next 3 dc, dc in next ch-1 sp, dc in joining, dc in corner ch-1 sp on **next** Square, (skip next 3 dc, 3 dc in sp **before** next dc) 4 times; repeat from ★ across to within 3 dc of next corner ch-1 sp, skip next 3 dc †, (3 dc, ch 1, 3 dc) in corner ch-1 sp, repeat from † to † once; join with slip st to first dc, finish off.

Rnd 2: With **right** side facing and holding strip vertically, join Tan with slip st in top right corner ch-1 sp; ch 3, (2 dc, ch 1, 3 dc) in same sp, (skip next 3 dc, 3 dc in sp **before** next dc) across to within 3 dc of next corner ch-1 sp, ★ skip next 3 dc, (3 dc, ch 1, 3 dc) in corner ch-1 sp, (skip next 3 dc, 3 dc in sp **before** next dc) across to within 3 dc of next corner ch-1 sp; repeat from ★ around, skip last 3 dc; join with slip st to first dc, finish off.

ASSEMBLY

With Tan, whipstitch Strips together, beginning in ch of first corner and ending in ch of next corner.

BORDER

Rnd 1: With **right** side facing and holding afghan vertically, join Tan with slip st in top right corner ch-1 sp; ch 3, 2 dc in same sp, † (skip next 3 dc, 3 dc in sp **before** next dc) 6 times, ★ skip next 3 dc, dc in next ch-1 sp, dc in joining, dc in next ch-1 sp on **next** Strip, (skip next 3 dc, 3 dc in sp **before** next dc) 6 times; repeat from ★ across to within 3 dc of next corner, skip next 3 dc, (3 dc, ch 1, 3 dc) in corner ch-1 sp, (skip next 3 dc, 3 dc in sp **before** next dc) across to within 3 dc of next corner, skip next 3 dc †, (3 dc, ch 1, 3 dc) in corner ch-1 sp, repeat from † to † once, 3 dc in same sp as first dc, sc in first dc to form last sp.

Rnd 2: Ch 3, 2 dc in same sp, (skip next 3 dc, 3 dc in sp before **next** dc) across to within 3 dc of next corner ch-1 sp, ★ skip next 3 dc, (3 dc, ch 1, 3 dc) in corner ch-1 sp, (skip next 3 dc, 3 dc in sp **before** next dc) across to within 3 dc of next corner ch-1 sp; repeat from ★ 2 times **more**, 3 dc in same sp as first dc, sc in first dc to form last sp.

Rnd 3: Ch 1, 3 sc in same sp, sc in each dc across to next corner ch-1 sp, ★ 3 sc in corner ch-1 sp, sc in each dc across to next corner ch-1 sp; repeat from ★ 2 times **more**; join with slip st to first dc, finish off.

City Blocks

Instructions continued from page 12

BORDER

Rnd 1: With **right** side facing, join Dk Brown with slip st in any corner ch-3 sp; ch 3, (dc, ch 2, 2 dc) in same sp, ★ skip next dc, dc in next 4 dc, (ch 1, dc in next dc) 3 times, ch 1, dc in next 4 dc, skip next dc, † dc in next ch-sp, dc in joining, dc in next ch-sp on **next** Square, skip next dc, dc in next 4 dc, (ch 1, dc in next dc) 3 times, ch 1, dc in next 4 dc, skip next dc †, repeat from † to † across to next corner ch-3 sp, (2 dc, ch 2, 2 dc) in corner ch-3 sp; repeat from ★ 2 times **more**, skip next dc, dc in next 4 dc, (ch 1, dc in next dc) 3 times, ch 1, dc in next 4 dc, skip next dc, repeat from † to † across; join with slip st to first dc.

Rnd 2: Ch 1, sc in same st and in next dc, 5 sc in corner ch-2 sp, ★ sc in each sc and in each ch-1 sp across to next corner ch-2 sp, 5 sc in corner ch-2 sp; repeat from ★ 2 times **more**, sc in each sc and in each ch-1 sp across; join with slip st to first sc, finish off.

Star Spangled

Instructions continued from page 15

Rnd 5: With **right** side facing, join Blue with slip st in any corner ch-2 sp; ch 1, (2 sc, ch 2, 2 sc) in same sp, sc in each st and in each ch-1 sp across to next corner ch-2 sp, ★ (2 sc, ch 2, 2 sc) in corner ch-2 sp, sc in each st and in each ch-1 sp across to next corner ch-2 sp; repeat from ★ 2 times **more**; join with slip st to first sc, finish off.

Rnd 6: With **right** side facing, join Red with slip st in any corner ch-2 sp; ch 3 **(counts as first dc, now and throughout)**, (dc, ch 2, 2 dc) in same sp, dc in next 8 sc, work FPtr around st **below** each of next 3 sc, dc in next 8 sc, ★ (2 dc, ch 2, 2 dc) in corner ch-2 sp, dc in next 8 sc, work FPtr around st **below** each of next 3 sc, dc in next 8 sc; repeat from ★ 2 times **more**; join with slip st to first dc, finish off.

ASSEMBLY

With Red, whipstitch Squares together, forming 8 vertical strips of 9 Squares each **(Fig. 3, page 34)**, beginning in second ch of first corner and ending in first ch of next corner; then whipstitch strips together in same manner.

BORDER

Rnd 1: With **right** side facing, join Red with slip st in any corner ch-2 sp; ch 3, 2 dc in same sp, dc in each st, ch-sp, and joining across to next corner ch-2 sp, ★ 3 dc in corner ch-2 sp, dc in each st, ch-sp, and joining across to next corner ch-2 sp; repeat from ★ 2 times **more**; join with slip st to first dc.

Rnd 2: Ch 1, sc in same st, 3 sc in next dc, ★ sc in each dc across to center dc of next corner, 3 sc in corner dc; repeat from ★ 2 times **more**, sc in each dc across; join with slip st to first sc, finish off.

Paintbox

Finished Size: 40" w x 52" l (101.5 x 132) cm

MATERIALS

Medium Weight Yarn
[7 ounces, 364 yards
(198 grams, 333 meters) per skein]:
Black - 4 skeins
Yellow - 1 skein
Hot Pink - 1 skein
Turquoise - 1 skein
[5 ounces, 232 yards (141 grams, 212 meters)
per skein]:
Lime - 2 skeins
Crochet hook, size F (3.75 mm) **or** size needed
for gauge
Tapestry needle

GAUGE: Each Square = 4" (10 cm)

STITCH GUIDE

**FRONT POST DOUBLE TREBLE CROCHET
(abbreviated FPdtr)**
YO 3 times, insert hook from **front** to **back**
around post of st indicated **(Fig. 1, page 34)**,
YO and pull up a loop (5 loops on hook), (YO
and draw through 2 loops on hook) 4 times.
Skip st behind FPdtr.

SQUARE (Make 63)

Make 16 Squares each with Main Color of Lime,
Turquoise, and Hot Pink; make 15 Squares with
Yellow.

With Main Color, ch 10; join with slip st to form
a ring.

Rnd 1 (Right side)**:** Ch 4 (**counts as first dc plus
ch 1**), (dc in ring, ch 1) 15 times; join with slip st to
first dc: 16 dc and 16 ch-1 sps.

Loop a short piece of yarn around any stitch to
mark Rnd 1 as **right** side.

Rnd 2: Slip st in first ch-1 sp, ch 6 (**counts as first
dc plus ch 3**), ★ dc in next ch-1 sp, (ch 1, dc in next
ch-1 sp) 3 times, ch 3; repeat from ★ 2 times
more, (dc in next ch-1 sp, ch 1) 3 times; join with
slip st to first dc.

Rnd 3: Slip st in first ch-3 sp, ch 3 (**counts as first
dc, now and throughout**), (3 dc, ch 2, 4 dc) in
same sp, (ch 1, dc in next ch-1 sp) 3 times, ch 1,
★ (4 dc, ch 2, 4 dc) in next ch-3 sp, (ch 1, dc in
next ch-1 sp) 3 times, ch 1; repeat from ★ 2 times
more; join with slip st to first dc, finish off.

Rnd 4: With **right** side facing, join Black with
slip st in any corner ch-2 sp; ch 3, (dc, ch 3, 2 dc)
in same sp, skip next dc, dc in next 3 dc, (ch 1, dc
in next dc) 3 times, ch 1, dc in next 3 dc, ★ skip
next dc, (2 dc, ch 3, 2 dc) in corner ch-3 sp, skip
next dc, dc in next 3 dc, (ch 1, dc in next dc) 3
times, ch 1, dc in next 3 dc; repeat from ★ 2 times
more, skip last dc; join with slip st to first dc,
finish off.

Rnd 5: With **right** side facing, join Main Color with slip st in any corner ch-3 sp; ch 3, (dc, ch 3, 2 dc) in same sp, skip next dc, dc in next dc, work FPdtr around second dc to **left** of corner ch-2 sp on Rnd 3, work FPdtr around next dc on Rnd 3, dc in next dc on Rnd 4, (ch 1, dc in next dc) 4 times, work FPdtr around third dc to **right** of corner ch-2 sp on Rnd 3, work FPdtr around next dc on Rnd 3, dc in next dc, ★ skip next dc, (2 dc, ch 3, 2 dc) in corner ch-3 sp, skip next dc, dc in next dc, work FPdtr around second dc to **left** of corner ch-2 sp on Rnd 3, work FPdtr around next dc on Rnd 3, dc in next dc on Rnd 4, (ch 1, dc in next dc) 4 times, work FPdtr around third dc to **right** of corner ch-2 sp on Rnd 3, work FPdtr around next dc on Rnd 3, dc in next dc; repeat from ★ 2 times **more**, skip last dc; join with slip st to first dc, finish off.

21

Instructions continued on page 28

Baby's Favorite

Finished Size: 31¹/₂" x 36" (80 x 91.5) cm

MATERIALS

Medium Weight Yarn
[7 ounces, 364 yards
(198 grams, 333 meters) per skein**]**:
White - 2 skeins
Pink - 1 skein
Mint Green - 1 skein
Crochet hook, size F (3.75 mm) **or** size needed
for gauge
Tapestry needle

GAUGE: Each Square = 3¹/₄" (8.25 cm)

STITCH GUIDE

TRIPLE TREBLE CROCHET
(abbreviated tr tr)
YO 4 times, insert hook in st or sp indicated,
YO and pull up a loop (6 loops on hook), (YO
and draw through 2 loops on hook) 5 times.

SQUARE (Make 50)

With White, ch 4; join with slip st to form a ring.

Rnd 1 (Right side)**:** Ch 3 **(count as first dc, now
and throughout)**, 2 dc in ring, ch 1, (3 dc in ring,
ch 1) 3 times; join with slip st to first dc, finish off.

Loop a short piece of yarn around any stitch to
mark Rnd 1 as **right** side.

Rnd 2: With **right** side facing, join Mint Green with
slip st in any corner ch-1 sp; ch 3, (2 dc, ch 1,
3 dc) in same sp, (3 dc, ch 1, 3 dc) in each of next
3 ch-1 sps; join with slip st to first dc, finish off.

Rnd 3: With **right** side facing, join Pink with slip st
in any corner ch-1 sp; ch 3, 2 dc in same sp,
working in **front** of previous rnds and between
3-dc groups on Rnd 1, tr tr in beginning ring, 3 dc
in same sp on Rnd 2, skip next 3 dc, 3 dc in sp
before next dc *(Fig. 2, page 34)*, ★ 3 dc in next
ch-1 sp, working in **front** of previous rnds and
between 3-dc groups on Rnd 1, tr tr in beginning
ring, 3 dc in same sp on Rnd 2, skip next 3 dc,
3 dc in sp **before** next dc; repeat from ★ 2 times
more; join with slip st to first dc, finish off.

Rnd 4: With **right** side facing, join White with
slip st in any tr tr, ch 3, (2 dc, ch 1, 3 dc) in same
st, (skip next 3 dc, 3 dc in sp **before** next dc)
twice, ★ skip next 3 dc, (3 dc, ch 1, 3 dc) in next tr
tr, (skip next 3 dc, 3 dc in sp **before** next dc) twice;
repeat from ★ 2 times **more**, skip last 3 dc; join
with slip st to first dc, finish off.

SQUARE ASSEMBLY

With White, whipstitch Squares together, forming
5 vertical strips of 10 Squares each *(Fig. 3,
page 34)*, beginning in ch of first corner and
ending in ch of next corner.

STRIP BORDER

Rnd 1: With **right** side facing and holding strip vertically, join White with slip st in top right corner ch-1 sp; ch 3, (2 dc, ch 1, 3 dc) in same sp, † (skip next 3 dc, 3 dc in sp **before** next dc) 3 times, skip next 3 dc, (3 dc, ch 1, 3 dc) in corner ch-1 sp, (skip next 3 sts, 3 dc in sp **before** next dc) 3 times, ★ skip next 3 dc, dc in next ch-1 sp, dc in joining, dc in corner ch-1 sp on **next** Square, (skip next 3 dc, 3 dc in sp **before** next dc) 3 times; repeat from ★ across to within 3 dc of next corner ch-1 sp, skip next 3 dc †, (3 dc, ch 1, 3 dc) in corner ch-1 sp, repeat from † to † once; join with slip st to first dc, finish off.

Rnd 2: With **right** side facing and holding strip vertically, join Mint Green with slip st in top right corner ch-1 sp; ch 3, (2 dc, ch 1, 3 dc) in same sp, (skip next 3 dc, 3 dc in sp **before** next dc) across to within 3 dc of next corner ch-1 sp, ★ skip next 3 dc, (3 dc, ch 1, 3 dc) in corner ch-1 sp, (skip next 3 dc, 3 dc in sp **before** next dc) across to within 3 dc of next corner ch-1 sp; repeat from ★ around to last 3 dc, skip last 3 dc; join with slip st to first dc, finish off.

23

Instructions continued on page 28

With a Passion!

INTERMEDIATE

Finished Size: 39" w x 53" l (99 x 134.5) cm

MATERIALS

Medium Weight Yarn **(4 MEDIUM)**
[7 ounces, 364 yards
  (198 grams, 333 meters) per skein]:
  Purple - 4 skeins
  Lavender - 2 skeins
  White - 2 skeins
Crochet hook, size F (3.75 mm) **or** size needed
  for gauge
Tapestry needle

GAUGE: Each Square = 4³/₄" (12 cm)

STITCH GUIDE

FRONT POST TREBLE CROCHET
(abbreviated FPtr)
YO twice, insert hook from **front** to **back**
around post of st indicated *(Fig. 1, page 34)*,
YO and pull up a loop (4 loops on hook), (YO
and draw through 2 loops on hook) 3 times.

SQUARE (Make 88)

With Purple, ch 5; join with slip st to form a ring.

Rnd 1 (Right side)**:** Ch 3 **(counts as first dc, now
and throughout)**, 3 dc in ring, (ch 3, 4 dc in ring)
3 times, ch 1, hdc in first dc to form last sp: 16 dc
and 4 ch-3 sps.

Loop a short piece of yarn around any stitch to
mark Rnd 1 as **right** side.

Rnd 2: Ch 3, 3 dc in same sp, ★ ch 1, (4 dc, ch 3,
4 dc) in next ch-3 sp; repeat from ★ 2 times **more**,
ch 1, 4 dc in same sp as first dc, ch 3; join with
slip st to first dc, finish off.

Rnd 3: With **right** side facing, join Lavender with
slip st in any corner ch-3 sp, ch 3, (3 dc, ch 3,
4 dc) in same sp, ch 1, 4 dc in next ch-1 sp,
★ ch 1, (4 dc, ch 3, 4 dc) in next ch-3 sp, ch 1,
4 dc in next ch-1 sp; repeat from ★ 2 times **more**,
ch 1, skip last 4 dc; join with slip st to first dc,
finish off.

Rnd 4: With **right** side facing, join White with
slip st in any corner ch-3 sp; ch 3, (3 dc, ch 3,
4 dc) in same sp, (ch 1, 4 dc in next ch-1 sp) twice,
★ ch 1, skip next 4 dc, (4 dc, ch 3, 4 dc) in next
ch-3 sp, (ch 1, 4 dc in next ch-1 sp) twice; repeat
from ★ 2 times **more**, ch 1; join with slip st to first
dc, finish off.

Rnd 5: With **right** side facing, join Purple with
slip st in first dc to **left** of any corner ch-3 sp;
ch 1, sc in same st and in next 2 dc, ★ † work FPtr
around second dc to **left** of corner ch-3 sp on
Rnd 3, work FPtr around next dc on Rnd 3, skip
next dc and next ch-1 sp on Rnd 4, skip next dc,
sc in next 3 dc and in next ch-1 sp, sc in next 3 dc,
work FPtr around third dc to **right** of corner
ch-3 sp on Rnd 3, work FPtr around next dc on
Rnd 3, skip next dc and next ch-1 sp on Rnd 4,
skip next dc, sc in next 3 dc, 3 sc in corner
ch-3 sp †, sc in next 3 dc; repeat from ★ 2 times
more, then repeat from † to † once; join with
slip st to first sc, finish off.

Instructions continued on page 29

Hugs & Kisses

■■■□ **INTERMEDIATE**

Finished Size: 31¹/₂" w x 36¹/₄" l (80 x 92) cm

MATERIALS

Medium Weight Yarn 🧶 **④**
[7 ounces, 364 yards
(198 grams, 333 meters) per skein]:
Yellow - 3 skeins
Lt Blue - 2 skeins
Crochet hook, size F (3.75 mm) **or** size needed
for gauge
Tapestry needle

GAUGE: Each Square = 4³/₄" (12 cm)

STITCH GUIDE

TRIPLE TREBLE CROCHET
(abbreviated tr tr)
YO 4 times, insert hook in st or sp indicated,
YO and pull up a loop (6 loops on hook), (YO
and draw through 2 loops on hook) 5 times.

SQUARE (Make 42)

With Yellow, ch 4; join with slip st to form a ring.

Rnd 1 (Right side)**:** Ch 3 **(count as first dc, now
and throughout)**, 2 dc in ring, (ch 1, 3 dc in ring)
3 times, sc in first dc to form last sp.

Loop a short piece of yarn around any stitch to
mark Rnd 1 as **right** side.

Rnd 2: Ch 3, 2 dc in same sp, (3 dc, ch 1, 3 dc) in
each of next 3 ch-1 sps, 3 dc in same sp as first st,
ch 1; join with slip st to first dc, finish off.

Rnd 3: With **right** side facing, join Lt Blue with
slip st in any corner ch-1 sp; ch 3, 2 dc in same
sp, working in **front** of previous rnds and **between**
3-dc groups on Rnd 1, tr tr in beginning ring, 3 dc
in same sp on Rnd 2, skip next 3 dc, 3 dc in sp
before next dc **(Fig. 2, page 34)**, ★ 3 dc in next
ch-1 sp, working in **front** of previous rnds and
between 3-dc groups on Rnd 1, tr tr in beginning
ring, 3 dc in same sp on Rnd 2, skip next 3 dc,
3 dc in sp **before** next dc; repeat from ★ 2 times
more; join with slip st to first dc, finish off.

Rnd 4: With **right** side facing, join Yellow with
slip st in any tr tr, ch 3, 2 dc in same st, (skip next
3 dc, 3 dc in sp **before** next dc) twice, ★ skip next
3 dc, (3 dc, ch 1, 3 dc) in next tr tr, (skip next 3 dc,
3 dc in sp **before** next dc) twice; repeat from ★
2 times **more**, skip last 3 dc, 3 dc in same st as
first dc, sc in first dc to form last sp.

Rnd 5: Ch 3, 2 dc in same sp, (skip next 3 dc,
3 dc in sp **before** next dc) 3 times, ★ skip next
3 dc, (3 dc, ch 1, 3 dc) in next ch-1 sp, (skip next
3 dc, 3 dc in sp **before** next dc) 3 times; repeat
from ★ 2 times **more**, skip last 3 dc, 3 dc in same
sp as first dc, ch 1; join with slip st to first dc,
finish off.

Rnd 6: With **right** side facing, join Lt Blue with slip st in any corner ch-1 sp; ch 3, working in **front** of previous rnds, tr tr in center dc of 3-dc group to **right** of corresponding corner ch-1 sp on Rnd 3, 3 dc in same sp on Rnd 5, tr tr in center dc of 3-dc group to **left** of same corner ch-1 sp on Rnd 3, dc in same sp on Rnd 5, (skip next 3 dc, 3 dc in sp **before** next dc) 4 times, ★ skip next 3 dc, dc in next ch-1 sp, working in **front** of previous rnds, tr tr in center dc of 3-dc group to **right** of corresponding corner ch-1 sp on Rnd 3, 3 dc in same sp on Rnd 5, tr tr in center dc of 3-dc group to **left** of same corner ch-1 sp on

Rnd 3, dc in same sp on Rnd 5, (skip next 3 dc, 3 dc in sp **before** next dc) 4 times; repeat from ★ 2 times **more**, skip last 3 dc; join with slip st to first dc, finish off.

ASSEMBLY

With Lt Blue, whipstitch Squares together, forming 6 vertical strips of 7 Squares each *(Fig. 3, page 34)*, beginning in center dc of first corner and ending in center dc of next corner; then whipstitch strips together in same manner.

 Instructions continued on page 29

Instructions continued from page 21

Instructions continued from page 23

Rnd 6: With **right** side facing, join Black with slip st in any corner ch-3 sp; ch 3, (dc, ch 3, 2 dc) in same sp, skip next dc, dc in next dc, work FPdtr around second dc to **left** of corner ch-4 sp on Rnd 4, dc in next 3 sts, (ch 1, dc in next dc) 3 times, ch 1, dc in next 3 sts, work FPdtr around second dc to **right** of corner ch-3 sp on Rnd 4, dc in next dc, ★ skip next dc, (2 dc, ch 3, 2 dc) in corner ch-3 sp, skip next dc, dc in next dc, work FPdtr around second dc to **left** of corner ch-4 sp on Rnd 4, dc in next 3 sts, (ch 1, dc in next dc) 3 times, ch 1, dc in next 3 sts, work FPdtr around second dc to **right** of corner ch-3 sp on Rnd 4, dc in next dc; repeat from ★ around, skip last dc; join with slip st to first dc, finish off.

Rnd 3: With Pink, repeat Rnd 2.

Rnd 4: With White, repeat Rnd 2.

STRIP ASSEMBLY

With White, whipstitch Strips together, beginning in ch of first corner and ending in ch of next corner.

BORDER

Rnd 1: With **right** side facing and holding aghan vertically, join White with slip st in top corner ch-1 sp; ch 3, (2 dc, ch 1, 3 dc) in same sp, † (skip next 3 dc, 3 dc in sp **before** next dc) 7 times, ★ skip next 3 dc, dc in next ch-1 sp, dc in joining, dc in next ch-1 sp on **next** Strip, (skip next 3 dc, 3 dc in sp **before** next dc) 7 times; repeat from ★ across to within 3 dc of next corner, skip next 3 dc, (3 dc, ch 1, 3 dc) in corner ch-1 sp, (skip next 3 dc, 3 dc in sp **before** next dc) across to within 3 dc of next corner, skip next 3 dc †, (3 dc, ch 1, 3 dc) in corner ch-1 sp, repeat from † to † once; join with slip st to first dc.

ASSEMBLY

With Black and using Placement Diagram as a guide (see right), whipstitch Squares together forming 7 vertical strips of 9 Squares each **(Fig. 3, page 34)**, beginning in center ch of first corner and ending in center ch of next corner; then whipstitch strips together in same manner.

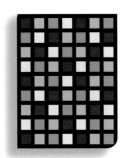

Rnd 2: Ch 1, sc in same st and in next 2 dc, 3 sc in corner ch-1 sp, ★ sc in each dc across to next corner ch-1 sp, 3 sc in corner ch-1 sp; repeat from ★ 2 times **more**, sc in each dc across; join with slip st to first dc, finish off.

BORDER

Rnd 1: With **right** side facing, join Black with slip st in any corner ch-3 sp; ch 3, (dc, ch 1, 2 dc) in same sp, dc in each dc, ch-sp, and joining across to next corner ch-3 sp, ★ (2 dc, ch 1, 2 dc) in corner ch-3 sp, dc in each dc, ch-sp, and joining across to next corner ch-3 sp; repeat from ★ 2 times **more**; join with slip st to first dc.

Rnd 2: Ch 1, sc in same st and in next dc, 3 sc in corner ch-1 sp, ★ sc in each dc across to next corner ch-1 sp, 3 sc in corner ch-3 sp; repeat from ★ 2 times **more**, sc in each dc across; join with slip st to first sc, finish off.

With a Passion!

Instructions continued from page 24

ASSEMBLY

With Purple, whipstitch Squares together forming 8 vertical strips of 11 Squares each *(Fig. 3, page 34)*, beginning in center sc of first corner and ending in center sc of next corner; then whipstitch strips together in same manner.

BORDER

Rnd 1: With **right** side facing, join Purple with slip st in center sc of any corner; ch 3, 2 dc in same st, dc in each st and in each joining across to center sc of next corner, ★ 3 dc in corner sc, dc in each st and in each joining across to center sc of next corner; repeat from ★ 2 times **more**; join with slip st to first dc.

Rnd 2: Ch 1, sc in same st, 3 sc in next dc, ★ sc in each dc across to center dc of next corner, 3 sc in corner dc; repeat from ★ 2 times **more**, sc in each dc across; join with slip st to first sc, finish off.

Hugs & Kisses

Instructions continued from page 27

BORDER

Rnd 1: With **right** side facing, join Lt Blue with slip st in center dc of any corner; ch 3, (2 dc, ch 1, 3 dc) in same st, ★ (skip next 3 sts, 3 dc in sp **before** next dc) 5 times, † skip next 3 sts, dc in next dc, dc in joining, dc in corner dc on **next** Square, (skip next 3 sts, 3 dc in sp **before** next dc) 5 times †, repeat from † to † across to within 3 sts of next corner st, skip next 3 sts, (3 dc, ch 1, 3 dc) in corner st; repeat from ★ 2 times **more**, (skip next 3 sts, 3 dc in sp **before** next dc) 5 times, repeat from † to † across to last 3 dc; join with slip st to first dc, finish off.

Rnd 2: With **right** side facing, join Yellow with slip st in any corner ch-1 sp; ch 3, 2 dc in same sp, (skip next 3 dc, 3 dc in sp **before** next dc) across to within 3 dc of next corner ch-1 sp, ★ skip next 3 dc, (3 dc, ch 1, 3 dc) in corner ch-1 sp, (skip next 3 dc, 3 dc in sp **before** next dc) across to within 3 dc of next corner ch-1 sp; repeat from ★ 2 times **more**, 3 dc in same sp as first dc, sc in first dc to form last sp.

Rnds 3 and 4: Ch 3, 2 dc in same sp, (skip next 3 dc, 3 dc in sp **before** next dc) across to within 3 dc of next corner ch-1 sp, ★ skip next 3 dc, (3 dc, ch 1, 3 dc) in corner ch-1 sp, (skip next 3 dc, 3 dc in sp **before** next dc) across to within 3 dc of next corner ch-1 sp; repeat from ★ 2 times **more**, 3 dc in same sp as first dc, sc in first dc to form last sp.

Rnd 5: Ch 1, 3 sc in first ch-1 sp, sc in each dc across to next corner ch-1 sp, ★ 3 sc in corner ch-1 sp, sc in each dc across to next corner ch-1 sp; repeat from ★ 2 times **more**; join with slip st to first sc, finish off.

Snow Days

Finished Size: 40" w x 51" l (101.5 x 129.5) cm

MATERIALS

Medium Weight Yarn
[7 ounces, 364 yards
   (198 grams, 333 meters) per skein]:
   Dk Green - 3 skeins
   Lt Green - 2 skeins
   Off White - 2 skeins
Crochet hook, size F (3.75 mm) **or** size needed
   for gauge
Tapestry needle

GAUGE: Each Square = 6¹/₄" (16 cm)

STITCH GUIDE

FRONT POST DOUBLE TREBLE CROCHET
   (abbreviated FPdtr)
YO 3 times, insert hook from **front** to **back**
around post of st indicated *(Fig. 1, page 34)*,
YO and pull up a loop (5 loops on hook), (YO
and draw through 2 loops on hook) 4 times.
Skip st behind FPdtr.

SQUARE (Make 48)

With Off White, ch 10; join with slip st to form
a ring.

Rnd 1 (Right side)**:** Ch 4 **(counts as first dc plus
ch 1)**, (dc in ring, ch 1) 15 times; join with slip st to
first dc: 16 dc and 16 ch-1 sps.

Loop a short piece of yarn around any stitch to
mark Rnd 1 as **right** side.

Rnd 2: Slip st in first ch-1 sp, ch 6 **(counts as first
dc plus ch 3)**, ★ dc in next ch-1 sp, (ch 1, dc in
next ch-1 sp) 3 times, ch 3; repeat from ★ 2 times
more, (dc in next ch-1 sp, ch 1) 3 times; join with
slip st to first dc, finish off.

Rnd 3: With **right** side facing, join Lt Green with
slip st in any corner ch-3 sp; ch 3 **(counts as first
dc, now and throughout)**, (3 dc, ch 2, 4 dc) in
same sp, (ch 1, dc in next ch-1 sp) 3 times, ch 1,
★ (4 dc, ch 2, 4 dc) in corner ch-3 sp, (ch 1, dc in
next ch-1 sp) 3 times, ch 1; repeat from ★ 2 times
more; join with slip st to first dc, finish off.

Rnd 4: With **right** side facing, join Dk Green with
slip st in any corner ch-2 sp; ch 3, (dc, ch 3, 2 dc)
in corner ch-2 sp, skip next dc, dc in next 3 dc,
(ch 1, dc in next dc) 3 times, ch 1, dc in next 3 dc,
★ skip next dc, (2 dc, ch 3, 2 dc) in corner ch-2 sp,
skip next dc, dc in next 3 dc, (ch 1, dc in next dc)
3 times, ch 1, dc in next 3 dc; repeat from ★ 2
times **more**, skip last dc; join with slip st to first dc,
finish off.

          Instructions continued on page 32